I  FLOWERS

STERLING CHILDREN'S BOOKS
New York

STERLING CHILDREN'S BOOKS
New York

An Imprint of Sterling Publishing Co., Inc.
122 Fifth Avenue
New York, NY 10011

ISBN 978-1-4549-4289-4

For information about custom editions, special sales, and premium and corporate purchases,
please contact Sterling Special Sales at 800-805-5489 or specialsales@sterlingpublishing.com.

Manufactured in China

Lot #:

2 4 6 8 10 9 7 5 3 1

12/20

sterlingpublishing.com

Design by Jack Clucas
Illustrated by Lizzie Preston and Jane Ryder-Gray
Additional material adapted from shutterstock.com

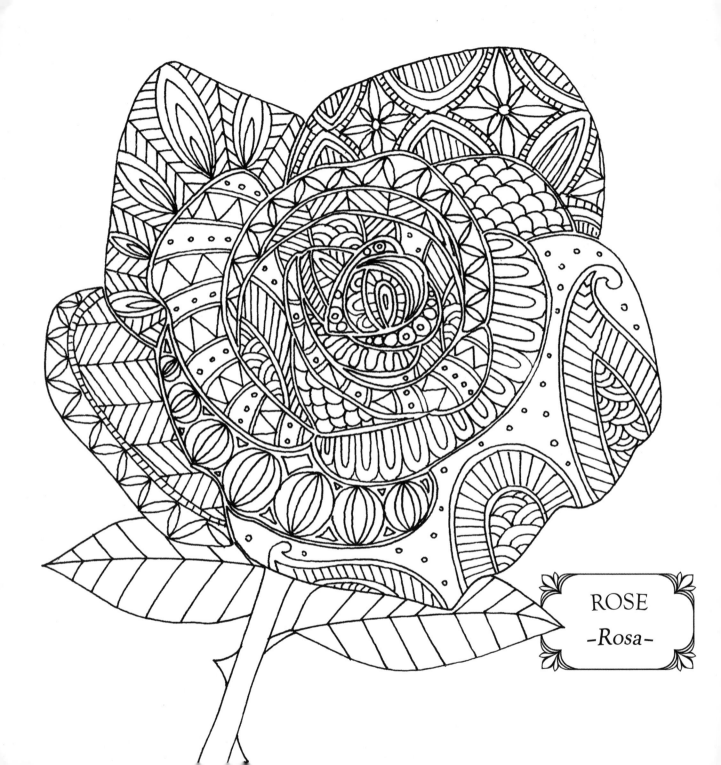

ROSE
-Rosa-

GERBERA

-Gerbera-

SNAPDRAGON
-Antirrhinum-

DAFFODIL
-Narcissus-

KING PROTEA
-Protea cynaroides-

LARKSPUR
-Delphinium consolida-

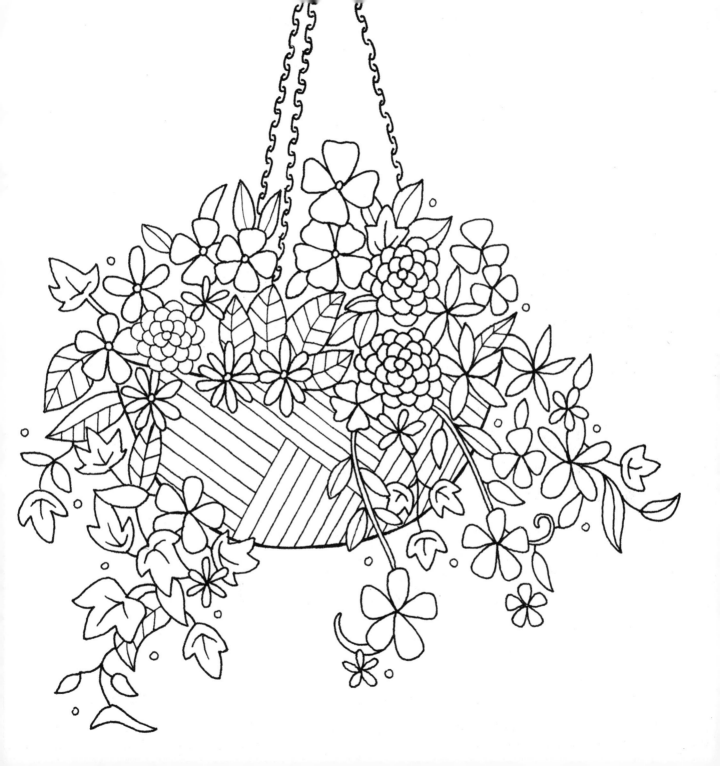

CHRYSANTHEMUM

-Chrysanthemum-

PHEASANT'S EYE
-Adonis annua-

LOVE-IN-A-MIST
-Nigella damascena-

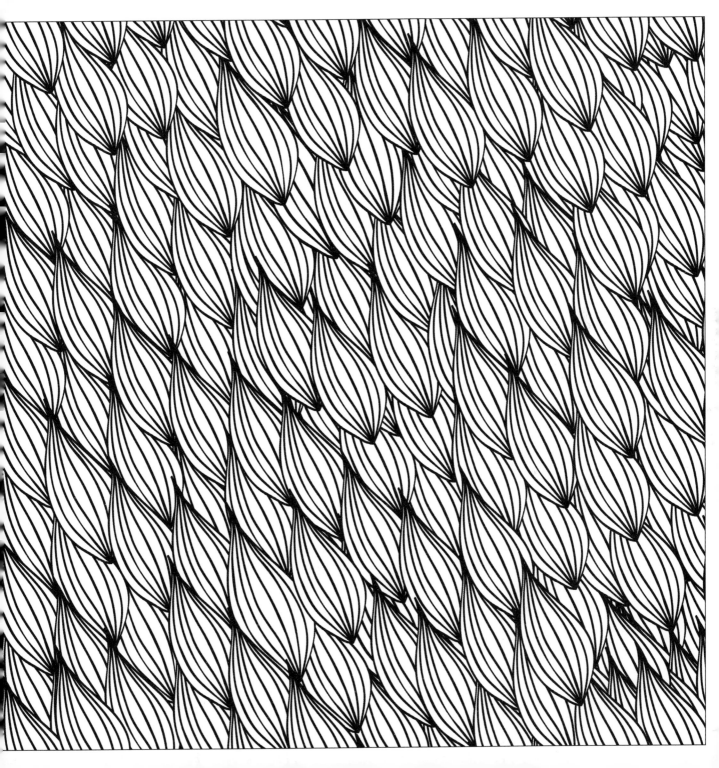

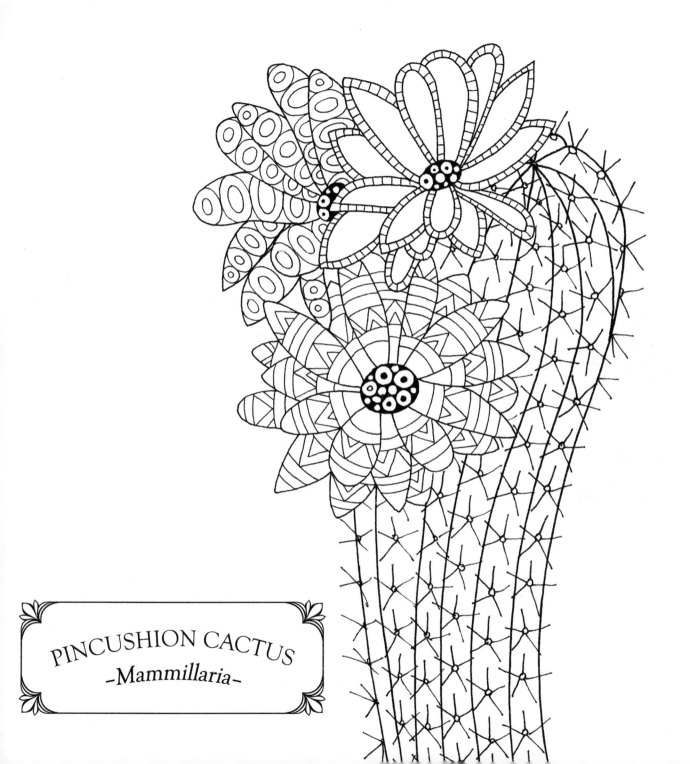

PINCUSHION CACTUS
-Mammillaria-

MOTH ORCHID
~Phalaenopsis~

LILY

-Lilium-

SACRED LOTUS
-Nelumbo nucifera-

BIRD-OF-PARADISE
-Strelitzia reginae-

PIMPERNEL
-Anagallis-

BELLFLOWER
-Campanula-

HYDRANGEA
-Hydrangea-

COLUMBINE
-Aquilegia-

LOBSTER CLAWS
-Heliconia-

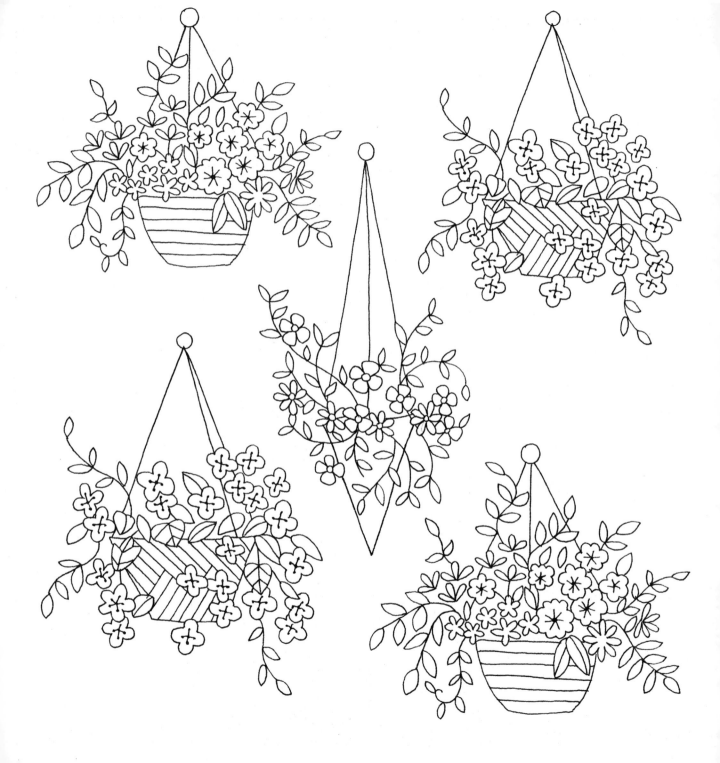

PASSION FLOWER
-Passiflora-

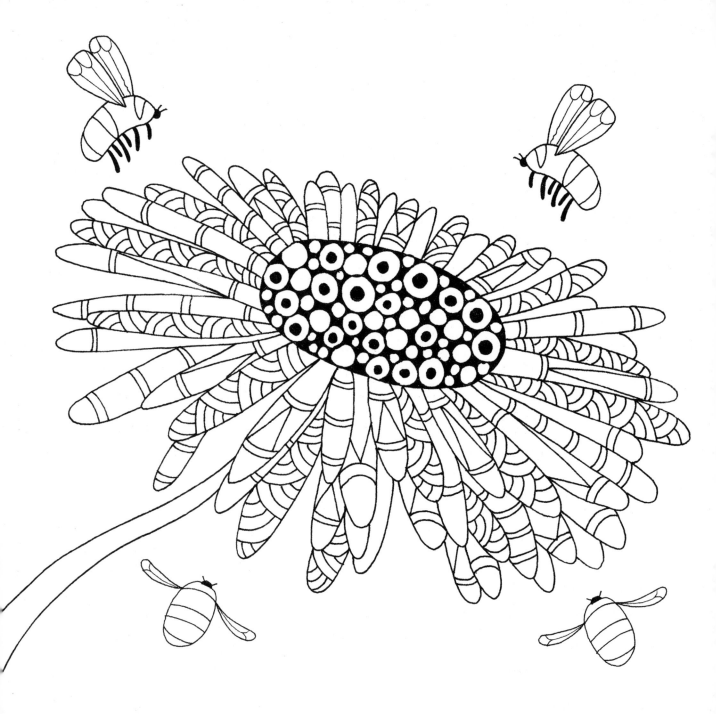

PERSIAN BUTTERCUP
-Ranunculus asiaticus-

PERUVIAN LILY

-Alstroemeria-

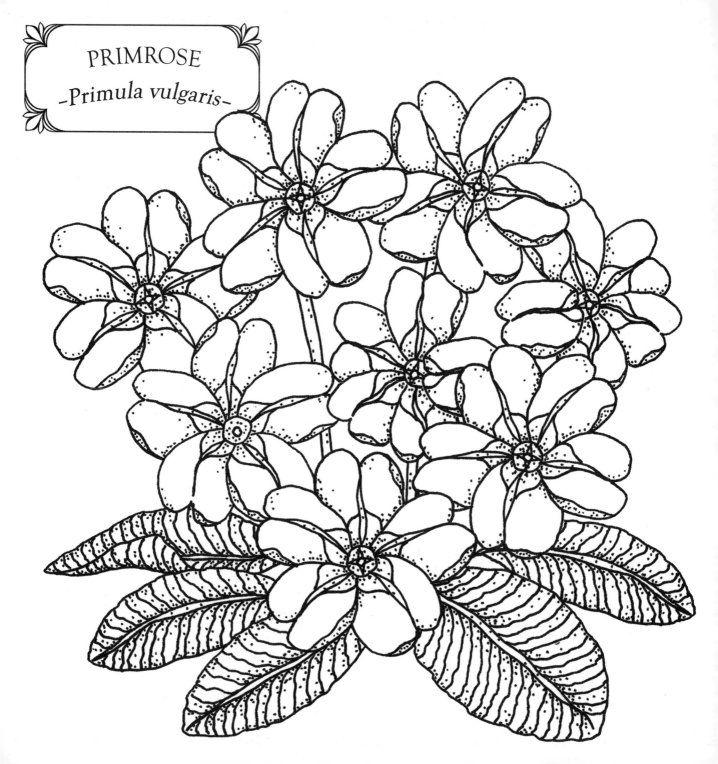

PRIMROSE

-Primula vulgaris-

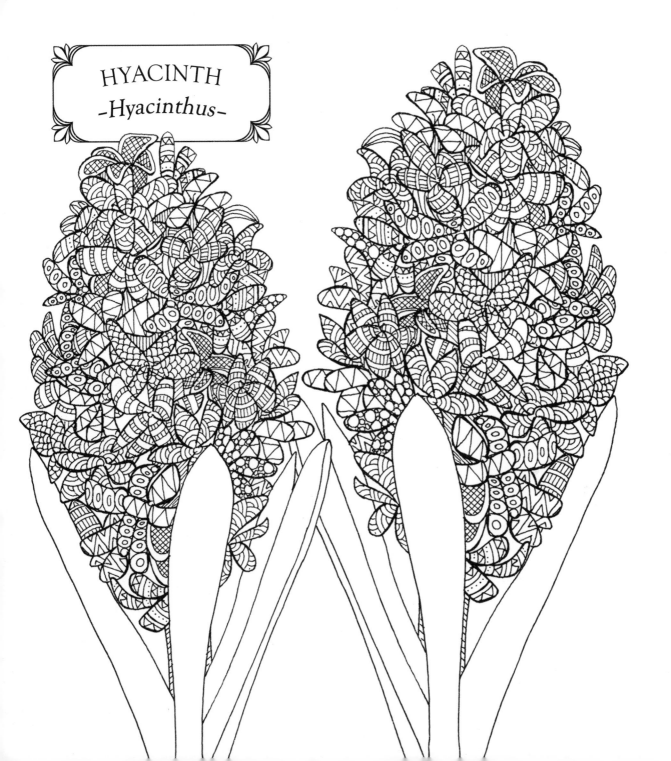

HYACINTH
-Hyacinthus-

FREESIA

–Freesia–

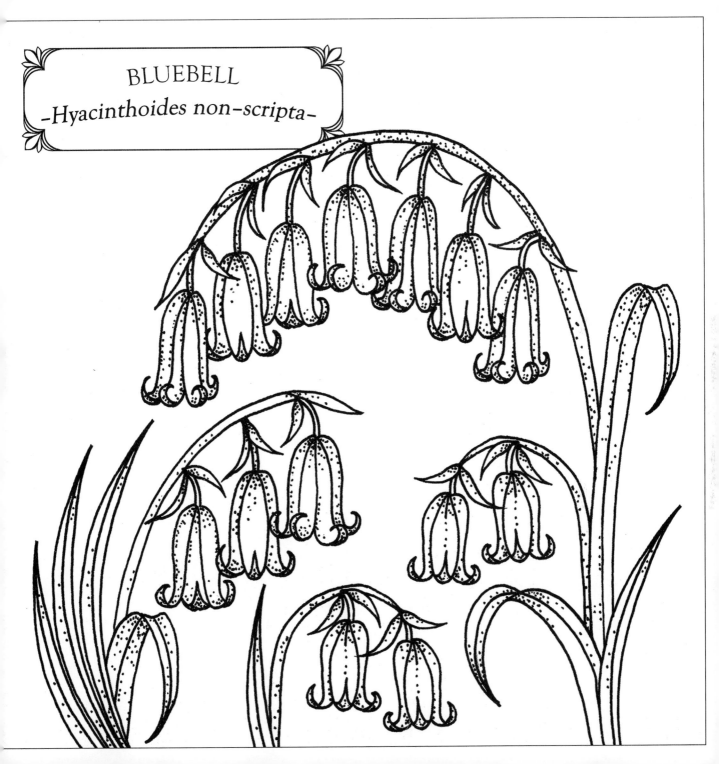

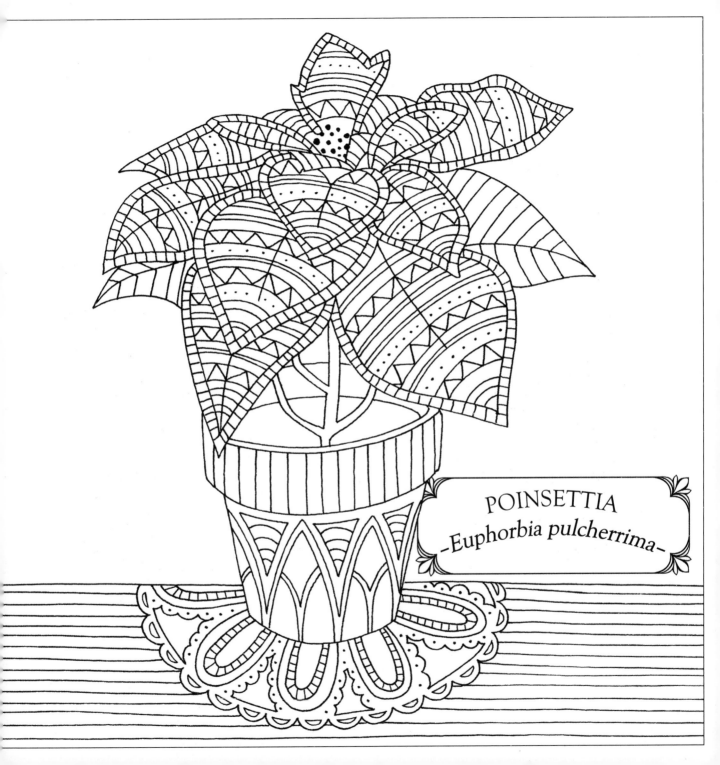

POINSETTIA
-Euphorbia pulcherrima-

SHEEP'S BIT

-Jasione montana-

WINDFLOWER
-Anemone-

TREASURE FLOWER
-Gazania linearis-

ANGELONIA
-Angelonia-

HIPPEASTRUM
-Hippeastrum-

DAHLIA
-Dahlia-

IRIS
-Iris-

CALLA LILY

-Zantedeschia-

PEONY

-Paeonia-